T0043342

BOBA
COOK
BOOK

BOBA COOK BOOK

Wendy Leung
Founder of Hello Always Tea

U

UNION
SQUARE
& CO.

NEW YORK

UNION
SQUARE
& CO.

NEW YORK

UNION SQUARE & CO. and the distinctive Union Square & Co. logo are
trademarks of Sterling Publishing Co., Inc.

Union Square & Co., LLC, is a subsidiary of Sterling Publishing Co., Inc.

Text © 2020 Wendy Leung
Photography © 2020 Sterling Publishing Co., Inc.

All rights reserved. No part of this publication may be reproduced,
stored in a retrieval system, or transmitted in any form or by any means
(including electronic, mechanical, photocopying, recording, or otherwise)
without prior written permission from the publisher.

ISBN 978-1-4549-4170-5
978-1-4549-4171-2 (e-book)

For information about custom editions, special sales, and premium purchases,
please contact specialsales@unionsquareandco.com.

Printed in Malaysia

4 6 8 10 9 7 5 3

unionsquareandco.com

Cover design by Jo Obarowski
Interior design by Shannon Nicole Plunkett

Photography by Rachel Johnson
Endpaper art by Livi from Oodles of Doodles/Creative Market

To my husband, Ray, who involuntarily accompanies me on all of my boba runs; thank you for indulging me on my bubble tea fantasies. You gave me the courage to quit my job, the confidence to open our own bubble tea shop, and the honor of naming our handsome German Shepherd Boba. You two are a daily reminder that life is great and when it's not, there's nothing a bubble tea can't fix.

CONTENTS

Introduction
HELLO, BOBA FRIENDS! • 8

Our Story • 10

Hello, Taiwan • 11

The Grind • 13

The Last Mile • 14

The Big Picture • 14

WHAT IS BUBBLE TEA? • 16

The Anatomy of Bubble Tea • 18

Know Your Bubble Tea • 19

Know Your Toppings • 21

A Note on Toppings • 22

Know Your Alternative Milks • 22

GETTING STARTED • 24

How to Brew Tea • 25

The Sweetness Test • 28

How to Make Tapioca • 31

How to Make Milk Foam • 41

THE RECIPES • 44

Milk Tea Series • 47

Fruit Tea Series • 59

Matcha Series • 71

Special Series • 79

Dessert Series • 87

Boba Party Series • 95

Conclusion
**GOODBYE,
BOBA FRIENDS! • 106**

Tea Resources • 107

Acknowledgments • 108

Index • 109

About the Author • 112

Introduction

HELL,
BBA
FRIENDS!

Thank you for sticking with us on our crazy adventure. Every person who has walked through the doors of my boba shop, Hello Always Tea, in New York City, or who attended a boba class, who came back again and again despite our ridiculous hours—this book is possible because of you. Your love and support fueled my boba dreams, and I am forever grateful.

To this day, I still get nervous whenever I meet someone who tries our bubble tea for the first time. It's scary not knowing what their immediate reaction will be, but there's no greater joy than to find someone who loves my recipes as much as I do. This is the reason why I started my bubble tea shop in the first place—sharing what I love most, my imperfectly perfect version of bubble tea.

As you embark on your own boba journey, remember that no two palates are the same. Use this book as a foundation for making your own, and tweak the recipes to accommodate your own tastes as you go. Channel your inner bobarista: the fun begins at the end of your comfort zone.

Thank you from the bottom of my heart.

Cheers,

Wendy

Our Story

Sometimes good things fall apart so that better things can fall together.
— MARILYN MONROE

t all started the moment when my husband (then boyfriend) Ray and I courageously quit our jobs. We had been living in San Francisco for three years, but we had been thinking about moving back home to the East Coast. We were both making six figures and I finally felt like my life was going in the right direction. I didn't grow up with money, so I felt incredibly lucky to be where I was. I was actually in the process of interviewing for a new job, which helped give us the push we needed to leave. Accepting a new job would mean staying for another year, and our hearts were no longer there in San Francisco. We were both ready for a new adventure and a well-deserved short vacation. Unbeknownst to us, our new endeavor would lead us to the opening of our very own bubble tea shop.

Looking back, it seems obvious that we made the right choice, but to be honest, quitting our jobs was one of the hardest decisions we had to make. I went down a rabbit hole of what-ifs and worst-case scenarios.

That kind of worrying and rationalizing was a game I was used to playing, and I was extremely good at losing and feeling overwhelmed. So as I debated whether or not to take the plunge, I found myself lost in another battle with myself, questioning my every decision.

The truth is, this wasn't the first time I let my irrational fears get to me. But as irrational as they were, my feelings were also valid. I was scared and anxious. And I couldn't stop myself from feeling this way: emotions just happen, and uncertainty really is scary. Obviously, it *was* a good idea after all—but at the time I had no idea! What I realize now is that things aren't always black and white, good or bad, or all or nothing. As cheesy as it sounds, change is a journey, and mine luckily has turned out to be a pretty great adventure.

Hello, Taiwan

We left San Francisco with a few bags and our white Hyundai Elantra. What followed was a month-long road trip back to New York. We watched sea lions in San Diego, hiked down the Grand Canyon, dug for diamonds in Arkansas, and had plenty of other exciting experiences, but our traveling didn't stop there. One month after reaching Ray's childhood home in New Jersey, we flew to Taiwan, the birthplace of bubble tea, for our much-anticipated vacation.

At last we were in boba heaven, surrounded by the best bubble tea shops in the world. So there I was, drinking what might have been my third bubble tea of the day, and a light bulb switched on. I turned to Ray and said, "We should open a bubble tea shop." He chuckled and looked at me expectantly. He was waiting for me to laugh back, because suggesting that we should open a shop was a stunt I had pulled before—but this time I wasn't joking. Our eyes met again, and we both knew that this time I genuinely meant what I was saying. I still have no idea what I said that day that convinced him to take me seriously, but it worked, and he was on board.

Believe me, I was just as surprised as he was. Opening a bubble tea shop was a daydream I'd had one too many times. I spent plenty of time joking with my old colleagues about opening one together, coming up with names for our imaginary shop, and dreaming about being the Starbucks of the bubble tea world.

> You can't connect the dots looking forward; you can only connect them looking backward.
>
> - STEVE JOBS

It was always a fun conversation to have, but each time, we eventually abandoned the thought as easily as we'd imagined it.

This time, I let my mind wander back to the idea of opening a bubble tea shop and considered it seriously. I'd already cycled through names, locations, and at least fifty imaginary setups. My daydreams tend to escalate quickly, so it wasn't long before I'd already built my boba empire. *Dream, delete, and repeat*—the unfortunate story of every daydream ever—but this time things would end differently. Turns out, one brave thing leads to another. First I quit my job, and because of that jump, opening a boba shop seemed like a cakewalk. Of course, it turned out to be much harder, but more on that later.

The important thing was that at some point I realized I was no longer daydreaming. I ended up in the place where dreams and reality collide, the absolute right place for taking steps to realize a lifelong dream. So we went to boba school, learned how to make bubble tea, and, in the name of research, traveled all over Taiwan, consuming all things boba.

The Grind

After three marvelous months in Taiwan, we flew back to New York with big dreams and new skills. Almost immediately, we started hunting for locations. Within two months, we had our eyes set on a small, humble space in the East Village. We excitedly put in an offer and thought that was it. *We did it; it's really happening.*

What naive children we were. Landlords are much more vigilant when it comes to first-time business ventures, and we had absolutely zero business experience at the time. Reasonably, they requested a business proposal. As an entrepreneurship major, I summoned everything I learned in college and composed a ten-page business plan. We had to prove we had the capital, a profitable business idea, and

six months of rent paid in advance, on top of an additional four months' security deposit. As abnormal as these terms seemed to us at the time, these were the obstacles every first-time business owner faces, and in those moments we were just grateful to be starting the process.

It took eight months of winning them over, making an offer, and negotiating the terms, but we finally came to an agreement. When the day came to sign the lease, I was as nervous as the day we signed our marriage certificate at city hall. It was that big a deal for me, because this was it—no turning back.

There is no magic to achievement. It's really about hard work, choices, and persistence.

- MICHELLE OBAMA

The Last Mile

Starting a business is a lot like running a marathon. We needed to give it everything we had on that very last mile, which, by the way, was the toughest part. So there we were with our brand new lease, and we hit the ground running. Find an architect, check. Design the shop, check. Import all the materials from Taiwan, check. We started with over thirty things on our to-do list, and the list continued to grow. To this day we are still working on it, because the reality is that once you start a business, the list doesn't stop.

Granted, there's always something to do, but the secret is to take it one day at a time. Build the shop, check. Buy furniture, check. Hire employees, check. Once I started seeing the to-do list as a friend, instead of a reminder of all of my responsibilities, my attitude shifted. What once was an overwhelming schedule had now become a reassuring agenda. I was gladly completing the tasks, because each item was a piece of the bigger picture. Train the employees, check. Finalize the menu, check. *Get ready for opening day, check!*

The Big Picture

It always seems impossible until it's done.
- NELSON MANDELA

Roll out the red carpet, pop the champagne, because we were open for business!

All the hard work from a year and a half of preparation led up to that very moment, our opening day. All of our family and friends came to support us, and it was one

> It's okay to be scared.
> Being scared means you're
> about to do something
> really, really brave.
> — MANDY HALE

of the most amazing days of our lives. We were so proud of what we accomplished, and to have them tell us the same was truly profound. It was the big picture we were hoping for, and every day, it has become much clearer. Every new boba friend who comes into our shop and tells us they love us for our bubble tea is a reminder of why we are here and why we love being a part of this community.

I'll be honest with you. I still get first-day jitters from time to time, especially when I'm trying something new. Then I go back and remember our opening day when we first opened our doors—I was actually so terrified that I hid behind the counter. I knew that the next moment was everything I worked hard for, and with that awareness I stood up for one final breath before unlocking the door. Deep breath in, deep breath out. I was

scared again, but this time it was different. This time I was different because I realized I'd changed.

Looking back over that year and a half, I realize that I faced more worry, unease, and doubt than I'd ever imagined, but through it all, I prevailed. I now carry those achievements with me, both wins and losses. As a matter of fact, the reminder that I can get back up after a loss is one of my greatest achievements.

Every day, I choose to look for happiness in whatever shape or form I can find. Sometimes it's the constant flow of joyful customers entering and leaving our shop, and other times it's hidden behind a slower day, when I get to bond with my staff. But no matter what, it always starts with one deep breath. Deep breath in, deep breath out. In those moments, I remember that there's so much to be grateful for.

WHAT IS BUBBLE TEA?

Did you know?

The "bubble" in bubble tea actually refers to the air bubbles formed by vigorously shaking the drink—though today we use the words *bubbles* and *tapioca* interchangeably.

Bubble tea started out as a simple drink made with milk tea and tapioca. Through time, and with the intent of creating better-tasting, visually appealing drinks, bubble tea now comes in many forms. We have milk teas, fruit teas, matcha, slushies, and brown sugar milk tea—just to name a few. What really makes it stand out are the different toppings we can include, like red bean, pudding, grass jelly, aloe vera, and more.

This distinction is what makes bubble tea such a fascinating drink as well as an exquisite dessert. We love this treat for its texture, its taste, and of course, the abundance of ways in which we can arrange it. Bubble tea is so versatile that there are innumerable ways to find, build, or design a drink that's right for everybody. The options are endless and will only continue to broaden as it transforms, diversifies, and innovates.

Bubble tea is a truly extraordinary drink, and once you step into this world, it will consume you. For better or worse, you will discover the best bubble tea, not just once but over and over again as you progress on your boba exploration. I'm warning you now: there will be nights when you will dream about your favorite bubble tea, and it will haunt you until that craving is satisfied. The good news is, when you do get your hands on that wonderful drink, the wait will make it that much more gratifying.

The Anatomy of Bubble Tea

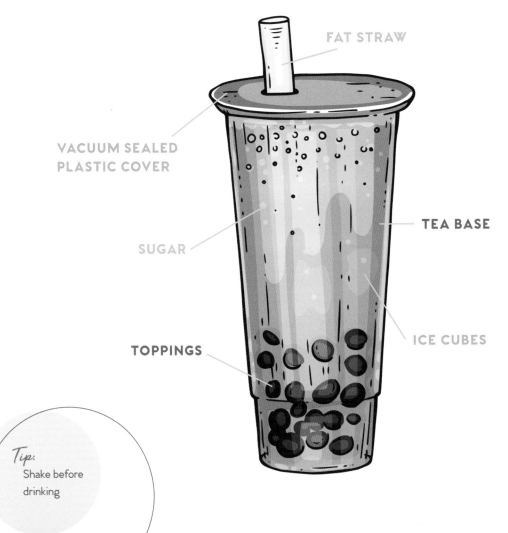

FAT STRAW

VACUUM SEALED
PLASTIC COVER

SUGAR

TEA BASE

TOPPINGS

ICE CUBES

Tip:
Shake before
drinking

Know Your Bubble Tea

BUBBLE MILK TEA

Classic black tea made with milk
(or non-dairy creamer) and tapioca.

CHEESE TEA

Choice of tea topped with creamy milk
foam made with cream cheese.

BROWN SUGAR MILK TEA

Caramelized brown sugar syrup swirled
with fresh milk and tapioca.

TARO MILK TEA

Taro is a starchy root vegetable.
Commonly made with taro powder and
non-dairy creamer.

THAI MILK TEA

A blend of black tea and spices splashed
with half-and-half.

MATCHA LATTE

Choice of milk topped with matcha tea.

FRUIT TEA

Flavored syrup and/or real fruits mixed
with tea base.

YAKULT

Yakult is a probiotic fermented milk
drink that's usually paired with jasmine
green tea or fruit.

If you were bubble tea, YOU would be my FAVORITE flavor.

BOBA MOMENT

What does bubble tea mean to you?

_____

Know Your Toppings

TAPIOCA (MOST POPULAR)

Made from starch extracted from the cassava plant. Usually coated with brown sugar or honey. Different flavors available.

MINI PEARLS

Smaller size of tapioca. Best mixed with regular-size tapioca for the contrasting proportions.

PUDDING

Custard-like gelatin-style dessert known for its sweet and milky taste.

GRASS JELLY

Jell-O™-like texture known for its herbal taste.

ALOE VERA

Soft and clear gel-like substance from the plant of the same name. Known for its health benefits and chewy texture.

RED BEAN

Cooked adzuki red beans known for their soft and sweet texture.

JELLY

Made with real coconut meat or konjac. Jellies come in many different flavors. Most popular are lychee jelly, mango jelly, and rainbow jelly.

POPPING BOBA

Like its name, it bursts with fruit juices or syrups contained in a thin gel-like covering. Popular flavors are green apple, mango, lychee, and strawberry.

Sometimes ignored but totally necessary.

A Note on Toppings

Toppings are optional in most of our recipes, but they are a great addition to all of the drinks in this book. I highly recommend including them in every recipe, in fact, and in testing out different toppings and topping mixtures. For example, one popular topping combo is known as the "3Q trio," which consists of tapioca, egg pudding, and grass jelly.

The standard amount is around one-half cup of toppings per drink, but feel free to add as little or as much as you want.

Know Your Alternative Milks

Lactose intolerant? No problem—try some of these dairy-free options.

ALMOND MILK

Made by blending almonds with water. Best paired with jasmine green tea.

OAT MILK

Made by soaking and blending steel-cut oats or whole groats. Best paired with oolong tea.

SOY MILK

Plant-based drink made with soybeans and water. Best paired with green tea or black tea.

Tip: For a creamier milk tea, purchase these dairy-free options in their barista or creamer versions that are creamier and meant to be used in drinks.

Today's
GOOD MOOD
is sponsored by
BOBA.

GETTING STARTED

The fun begins now. Every great cup of bubble tea starts with a strong foundation. This is where you learn how to brew the perfect tea, discover your sugar-intake preference, and master the art of homemade tapioca. There are multiple variations just from these elements alone—each equally crucial to your understanding of what makes the perfect bubble tea for you.

How to Brew Tea

BOBA MOMENT

Try predicting your personal preference:

How strong do you like your tea?

Light, Normal, Strong

How sweet do you like your tea?

(0–100 percent)

_____

BREWING TEA IS A THREE-STEP PROCESS: boil water, pour over tea leaves, and steep. Pretty simple, right? As it should be—but the truth is, brewing great-tasting tea is much more complicated. As with all things in life, the simple things are the hardest to perfect, and steeping tea is no different. To brew the perfect tea, there are three important factors: volume, temperature, and brew time.

The "perfect tea" is different for everyone—some people prefer a lighter tea and others prefer a stronger aroma. I am part of the latter group. I love my tea strong and milky. This is the way I like to brew my tea, but that doesn't necessarily mean it's the right way for you. You'll have to find out what you like most about the tea you drink and adjust these directions to produce that result.

To start, first follow the instructions listed on the package (or refer to the chart listing popular teas and their brew times on the facing page). In general, most teas will use the following method. When you make boba, it's essential to test the base first and then adjust accordingly so that you start with the right tea for you. It's going to take a few tries, but you've got this. Let's get brewing!

STEP 1

How much loose tea should I use?

Each tea is slightly different. A good medium would be starting at 5g of tea leaves.

Tip: Adjust by adding or subtracting 1g at a time

STEP 2

How much water should I use and at what temperature?

Use 1 cup of water. Temperatures will vary depending on the type of tea. Use the chart on the facing page as a guide.

Tip: Always use 1 cup of water to reduce the number of sequences. Adjust by playing with the temperature. Try raising or lowering the temperature by 1–2 degrees at a time.

STEP 3

How long should I steep the tea?

As with temperature, it varies depending on the type of tea. Use the chart on the facing page as a guide.

Tip: Adjust by adding or subtracting the steeping time by 1–2 minutes at a time.

Tea Chart

(Per 1 cup water for iced drinks; use 1½ cups water for hot drinks)

TEA BASE	TEMPERATURE	STEEP TIME*	AMOUNT
White tea	175–180°F	1–3 minutes	1 tablespoon
Green tea	175–185°F	2–6 minutes	1½ tablespoons
Oolong tea	190–205°F	4–10 minutes	1½ tablespoons
Black tea	200–210°F	6–12 minutes	2 tablespoons
Chrysanthemum flowers	200–210°F	At least 8 minutes	2 tablespoons
Butterfly pea flowers	200–210°F	5–10 minutes	1 tablespoon

* The different steep times are determined by your preference of lighter or stronger tea.

Tip: If you're using tea bags, don't end with a squeeze. That's where the concentrate is, and also the bitterness! Gently take out the tea bags and enjoy!

The Sweetness Test

Sugar level is an essential part of a great bubble tea and, consequently, when you order bubble tea, there is an option to choose your sugar preference. The sugar levels start at zero percent (no added sugar) and go up to 100 percent (regular sweetness). Everyone's sweetness level is distinct, so you don't have to compromise your sugar intake to have bubble tea.

So the question is, how sweet are you? Here's a test to help you determine which sugar level will taste the best for you. Use this percentage going forward when making your own bubble tea.

INGREDIENTS

2 cups of your favorite brewed tea

Cane sugar

STEP 1

Freshly brew 2 cups of your favorite tea. Prepare 5 mugs and pour ¼ cup (60mL) of tea into each mug (there will be leftover tea).

STEP 2

Label each mug with one of the following percentages: 0 percent sugar, 25 percent sugar, 50 percent sugar, 75 percent sugar, and 100 percent sugar. Next, add the corresponding amount of cane sugar into each mug: none, ½ teaspoon, 1 teaspoon, 1½ teaspoons, and 2 teaspoons. Stir until the sugar dissolves.

STEP 3

Start tasting! Begin at 0 percent sugar and work your way up to 100 percent sugar. Keep testing forward and backward until you find a good fit. This is your standard sugar level and a good base for making your own bubble tea or when ordering outside.

Now that you narrowed your sugar preference through intervals of 25 percent, try adjacent intervals of 5 percent next. For example, my standard sugar level is 75 percent, so my next test would be 65 percent, 70 percent, 75 percent, 80 percent, 85 percent, and so forth. Use our sweetness test chart for reference.

I am
———————
sweet

Sweetness Test

SWEETNESS LEVEL	¼ CUP (60ML) BREWED TEA	SWEETNESS LEVEL	¼ CUP (60ML) BREWED TEA
100 percent	2 tablespoons (10g) sugar	85 percent	8.5g sugar
75 percent	1½ tablespoons (7.5g) sugar	80 percent	8g sugar
50 percent	1 tablespoon (5g) sugar	75 percent	7.5g sugar
25 percent	½ tablespoon (2.5g) sugar	70 percent	7g sugar
0 percent	none (0g)	65 percent	6.5g sugar

Tip: Use this sugar percentage when you order bubble tea. This is a good way to determine what is right for you. The sweetness level for each shop varies slightly, so always adjust to your own needs.

Adding sugar to your bubble tea

Now that you have your sugar preference, you can either add cane sugar directly to your tea or prepare simple syrup ahead of time for convenience. Use our sugar level chart for details on how much cane sugar or simple syrup to add to your drink.

Sugar Level
(for one cup of tea)

SWEETNESS LEVEL	CANE SUGAR	SIMPLE SYRUP
100 percent	8 teaspoons (40g) sugar	80mL
75 percent	6 teaspoons (30g) sugar	60mL
50 percent	4 teaspoons (20g) sugar	40mL
25 percent	2 teaspoons (10g) sugar	20mL
0 percent	none (0g)	0mL

HOW TO MAKE SIMPLE SYRUP

1 cup (240mL) water

1 cup cane sugar

• Gently heat water and sugar together in a saucepan and stir until the sugar is dissolved.

Make Ahead

To make more simple syrup, follow the instructions using 1 part water and 1 part sugar. Store in a sterile container in the refrigerator for up to one month.

How to Make Tapioca

Without tapioca, there would be no bubble tea. The chewy bubbles are what transform Taiwanese desserts into drinks and vice versa. Bubble tea is a fusion of dessert and beverage. Great tapioca is soft but not mushy, firm but not hard, and chewy but not rubbery. The bounciness in this lightly sweetened topping is what represents the iconic term "QQ." In Taiwan, Q translates to soft and chewy, and double Q means really chewy. It's an experience that first timers need to get used to, but for those who are adventurous and have an appetite for new things, you'll soon become an expert in eating and drinking at the same time.

TAPIOCA POWDER VS. TAPIOCA STARCH

Tapioca powder and tapioca starch are essentially the same things. There are a variety of options on the market that will include ingredients such as tapioca starch, tapioca starch and water, just tapioca, or organic cassava. All of these will work with our recipes.

CLASSIC TAPIOCA

This is the classic, basic recipe for tapioca balls. You can use this as a topping in any of the drinks found in this book.

PREP TIME
20 minutes

Serves 2

YOU WILL NEED
A mixing bowl,
a rolling pin
(optional),
a knife

⅜ cup (50g) tapioca powder

⅛ cup (30g) boiling hot water

1. In a mixing bowl, stir together the tapioca powder and the boiling hot water.

2. Knead the mixture to a dough-like texture (A).

3. Flatten the dough and spread out into a square measuring 4 inches by 4 inches (sprinkle tapioca powder on the bottom and top to prevent sticking). You can use your hands or a rolling pin (B).

4. Using a knife, cut the dough into long strips.

5. Cut each strip of dough into smaller pieces (C), and then roll each of those pieces into a ball about the size of a pea (1cm).

6. Continue cutting strips and rolling pieces into smaller balls until you have a bowl of tapioca balls (D). This should make about 100 balls.

A
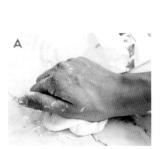

B

C

7. Cook immediately (see instructions that follow), or place in an airtight bag and store for up to six months in the freezer.

Tip: Make sure you are using the boiling hot water right away—if the water is not hot enough, the tapioca powder will turn into a weird but fun texture known as "Oobleck," a term for a substance that has properties of both a solid and liquid (kind of like quicksand or slime).

Time to cook them!

2¼ cups (700mL) water

½ cup (80g) uncooked tapioca balls

¼ cup (50g) brown sugar

¼ cup (60mL) hot water

1. Fill a pot with 2¼ cups (700mL) water and heat on high until the water is boiling.

2. Pour in the uncooked tapioca balls.

3. Stir continuously until all of the tapioca balls float to the top (about 1-2 minutes) **(E)**.

4. Cover with the lid and reduce the heat to medium-low.

5. Cook for 8 minutes, stirring occasionally.

6. Turn the heat off. Keeping the pot covered, wait another 8 minutes.

COOK TIME
40 minutes

Serves 2

YOU WILL NEED
A pot with a lid, a bowl

7. While waiting, make the syrup by mixing equal parts brown sugar and hot water in a bowl. Set it aside.

8. After 8 minutes, rinse the cooked tapioca balls under cold running water.

9. Pour the tapioca into the brown sugar syrup and stir to avoid clumping (F).

10. Let it soak for 10–15 minutes.

11. Serve immediately and enjoy! Tapioca tastes best when consumed within 2 hours.

F

Tip: If you're using dried, store-bought tapioca, the cooking and waiting time will double. This means a twenty-minute cook time followed by a twenty-minute wait time—which can bring the total time closer to an hour! It's a lot longer than you expected, right? Me too! Luckily, once you have this homemade boba in the fridge or freezer, it cooks up quickly, and you can keep it on hand for multiple batches of tea.

BROWN SUGAR SYRUP

¼ cup (60mL) hot water

¼ cup (50g) brown sugar

- Combine the ingredients in a small saucepan and cook until sugar is dissolved.

Note

– For frozen homemade tapioca, cook for 10 minutes and let cool for 10 minutes.

– If you're using dried, ready-made tapioca balls, cook for 20 minutes and let cool for 20 minutes.

– In both cases, you should still soak in brown sugar syrup for at 10–15 minutes.

homemade

store bought

Tapioca Variations!

Tapioca consists of only two ingredients—tapioca powder and water. The fascinating part is that you can alter the water by infusion to make flavored tapioca. How cool is that? Here are three flavored tapioca recipes for you to try.

Matcha Tapioca

This delicious variation incorporates green matcha powder.

⅜ cup (80g) tapioca powder

⅛ cup (48mL) boiling hot water

¼ teaspoon matcha powder

• Follow the instructions for classic tapioca. Add the extra ingredient, matcha powder, immediately after adding the hot water. Soak it with our honey brown sugar mix.

Note: This is best paired with the Matcha Latte recipe on page 73; it enhances each sip with mini-matcha magic!

HONEY BROWN SUGAR SYRUP

⅛ cup honey

⅛ cup (25g) brown sugar

¼ cup (60mL) hot water

• Combine the ingredients in a saucepan and cook until the sugar and honey are dissolved.

Rose Water Tapioca

Rose water is a delicious ingredient made by steeping rose petals in water. It can give your tapioca a lovely perfume.

1 cup (240mL) hot water

2 tablespoons (3g) rose petals (use for the rose water)

⅝ cup (85g) tapioca powder

1 tablespoon (1.5g) diced rose petals

Mixing bowl

PREP TIME
30 minutes

COOK TIME
40 minutes

Serves 3-4

YOU WILL NEED
Two bowls, a pot, a knife

1. Steep 2 tablespoons of rose petals with 1 cup of hot water for 3 minutes. Strain the rose petals (slightly less than a cup/about 200mL of rose water will remain). Reboil ¼ cup (60mL) of rose water in a saucepan (remember, we need boiling hot water to mix). Mix immediately with ½ cup tapioca powder. When it gets sticky, mix in another ⅛ cup of tapioca powder until you have a dough-like texture. Add in diced rose petals and follow the rest of the instructions for classic tapioca.

2. Use the remaining rose water to make rose water syrup.

ROSE WATER SYRUP

½ cup (120mL) rose water

¼ cup (50g) cane sugar

- Combine ingredients in a small saucepan and cook until sugar is dissolved.

Brown Sugar Tapioca

These are the black tapioca balls you may be familiar with, since they are the ones you'll see most often when getting boba from a bubble tea shop. These tapioca balls are already manufactured with dark brown sugar in them, which gives them their sparkling, opaque color. This recipe will add familiar color and brown sugar taste to your homemade tapioca balls.

⅜ cups (80g) tapioca powder

⅛ cup (48mL) hot water

⅛ cup (25g) dark brown sugar

PREP TIME
25 minutes

COOK TIME
45 minutes

Serves 2

YOU WILL NEED
A cutting board, a pot, a knife, a spatula

1. In a pot, add ⅛ cup water and ⅛ cup dark brown sugar. On low heat, stir until the sugar dissolves. Increase to medium heat and wait for it to boil. Turn off the heat and immediately add half of the tapioca powder. Mix with a spatula for 10 seconds and add the rest of the tapioca powder. Keep mixing until you have a dough.

2. Transfer the dough onto the cutting board and start kneading. Be careful; the dough is still hot.

3. Flatten the dough and spread out into a square measuring 4 inches by 4 inches (sprinkle tapioca powder on the bottom and on top to prevent sticking). You can use your hands or a rolling pin.

4. Using a knife, cut the dough into long strips.

5. Cut each strip of dough into smaller pieces and then roll each of those pieces into a ball about the size of a pea (1cm).

6. Continue cutting strips and rolling pieces into smaller balls until you have a bowl of tapioca balls. This should make about 100 balls.

7. Cook immediately (see the instructions for classic tapioca), or place in an airtight bag and store in the freezer for up to six months.

How to Make Milk Foam

Milk foam is the ideal middle ground between smooth milk and stiff whipped cream. The foam created by this process produces a lighter taste and mouthfeel than cream but keeps all of its rich flavor. Each sip of soft homemade milk foam will have you feeling like you're drinking tea in the clouds.

I've also included the recipes for some variations, including one that has become super popular: cheese milk foam.

CLASSIC MILK FOAM

PREP TIME
2 minutes

Serves 1

YOU WILL NEED
Bowl,
hand mixer
or blender

¼ cup heavy cream

3 tablespoons milk

2 teaspoons cane sugar

• Using a hand mixer, whip all the ingredients in a bowl until soft peaks form. Serve immediately.

CHEESE MILK FOAM

PREP TIME
2 minutes

Serves 1

YOU WILL NEED
Bowl, hand mixer
or blender

¼ cup heavy cream

3 tablespoons milk

2 teaspoons cane sugar

1 teaspoon cream cheese

A pinch of sea salt

• Using a hand mixer, whip all the ingredients in a bowl until soft peaks form. Serve immediately.

COCOA MILK FOAM

¼ cup heavy cream

3 tablespoons milk

2 teaspoons cane sugar

½ teaspoon cocoa
   powder

A pinch of sea salt

• Using a hand mixer,
whip all the ingredients
in a bowl until soft
peaks form. Serve
immediately.

PREP TIME

2 minutes

Serves 1

YOU WILL NEED
Bowl, hand
mixer or
blender

MATCHA MILK FOAM

PREP TIME

2 minutes

Serves 1

YOU WILL NEED
Bowl, hand mixer
or blender

¼ cup heavy cream

3 tablespoons milk

2 teaspoons cane
sugar

¼ teaspoon matcha
powder

• Using a hand mixer,
whip all the ingredients
in a bowl until soft peaks
form. Serve immediately.

CHARCOAL MILK FOAM

PREP TIME
2 minutes

Serves 1

YOU WILL NEED
Bowl,
hand mixer
or blender

¼ cup heavy cream

3 tablespoons milk

2 teaspoons cane sugar

½ teaspoon charcoal powder

⅛ teaspoon vanilla extract

- Using a hand mixer, whip all the ingredients in a bowl until soft peaks form. Serve immediately.

BUTTERFLY PEA MILK FOAM

¼ cup heavy cream

3 tablespoons milk

2 teaspoons cane sugar

1½ tablespoons butterfly pea tea leaves

- Add all the ingredients to a bowl. Cover and refrigerate for at least 4 hours. Stir the liquid and strain it to remove the tea leaves. Using a hand mixer, whip all the ingredients until soft peaks form. Serve immediately.

PREP TIME
2 minutes

COOK TIME
4 hours

Serves 1

YOU WILL NEED
Bowl, hand mixer
or blender,
strainer

THE
RECIPES

MILK TEA SERIES

Milk tea • 49

Bubble milk tea • 51

Milk foam • 52

Hong Kong milk tea • 53

Caramel milk tea • 55

Brown sugar milk tea • 57

FRUIT TEA SERIES

Passionfruit green tea • 61

Lemon tea • 62

Strawberry green tea • 63

Strawberry pop • 63

Lychee green tea • 64

Peach lime green tea • 67

Grapefruit green tea • 68

Grapefruit pop • 69

MATCHA SERIES

Matcha latte • 73

Matcha tea • 74

Charcoal matcha latte • 75

Matcha mojito • 77

SPECIAL SERIES

Yakult green tea • 81

Strawberry milk • 82

Strawberry matcha latte • 83

Strawberry lemonade • 85

DESSERT SERIES

Panna cotta • 88

Matcha affogato • 89

Fruity Pops • 91

Soufflé Pancakes • 92

BOBA PARTY SERIES

"When I grow up"
OREO POTTED PLANT MILK TEA • 97

"Secret Garden" FRUIT TEA • 99

"We Oolong Together"
LEMON HONEY OOLONG TEA • 101

"Legend of the Blue Sea"
BUTTERFLY PEA LEMONADE • 102

Step aside
coffee.
This is a job
for B●BA!

Milk Tea Series

Before bubble tea, there was milk tea—and I was hooked. I have been drinking it religiously since elementary school. Every day was the same routine: back in the '90s, my allowance was a dollar a day, which covered a cup of milk tea and a pastry at my local bakery. Occasionally, I switched it up and got two packs of gum and a candy bar.

Life was simple, a dollar was a lot of money, and milk tea was my favorite drink. Although life is more complicated now and money is confusing, I still enjoy milk tea on a regular basis. The solar system can change, but milk tea will stand the test of time.

Did you know?

Pluto used to be a planet. It got demoted to a dwarf planet in 2006.

MILK TEA

This recipe is the taste of my childhood and the base for bubble tea. Milk teas are great with all tea bases. After a bunch of experimentation at Hello Always Tea, we achieved the perfect balance with our milk-to-tea ratio. Too much milk can overpower the tea itself, and not enough milk barely makes it a milk tea. Our recipe has a proportion that helps milk and tea complement one another so that the result is both creamy and strong.

COOK TIME
5 minutes

Serves 1

YOU WILL NEED
Glass jar

Ice cubes

Simple syrup, to taste (see page 30)

1 cup brewed tea

⅛ cup (40mL) half-and-half

1. Put the ice cubes into the glass jar.

2. Add the simple syrup.

3. Add the brewed tea.

4. Slowly pour the half-and-half over an ice cube.

5. Stir and enjoy.

DAIRY-FREE OPTION Replace the milk with 50mL of alternative milk.

BEST PAIRED WITH Tapioca, pudding, or grass jelly

QUICK TIP Play with the milk ratio to see if more or less milk suits your taste.

BUBBLE MILK TEA

This is the original bubble tea and still a fan favorite: classic black milk tea
with tapioca. A blend of fresh milk swirled into this luscious black tea is
what gives it the perfect combination of creamy and strong tastes.

COOK TIME
5 minutes

Serves 1

YOU WILL NEED
Glass jar

½ cup (80g) cooked
tapioca (see page 51)

Ice cubes

Simple syrup, to taste
(see page 30)

1 cup brewed tea

⅛ cup (30mL)
half-and-half

1. Make 80g of cooked
   tapioca with Classic
   Tapioca Recipe on
   page 32.

2. Scoop the cooked tapioca
   into a glass jar.

3. Add the ice cubes.

4. Add the simple syrup.

5. Add the brewed tea.

6. Slowly pour the half-and-half over an ice cube.

7. Stir and enjoy!

MILK FOAM TEA

This drink goes by many names, but don't let the confusion intimidate you from trying milk tea's fluffy twin! As a base we have sweetened tea topped off with our homemade soft rich milk foam. Each sip will have you feeling like you're drinking tea in the clouds.

Ice cubes

Simple syrup, to taste
(see page 30)

1 cup brewed tea

½ cup (100mL) classic
milk foam
(see page 41)

1. Put the ice cubes into a glass jar.

2. Add the simple syrup.

3. Add the brewed tea and give it a quick stir.

4. Slowly add the milk foam over the ice to create the separate layer.

VARIATION Experiment with different tea bases and different milk foam flavors.

QUICK TIP Here are two ways to drink it: Sip from the side of the cup to get the contrasting taste, or mix it together for a creamy milk tea with a salty kickback!

Names for the drink according to different bubble tea shops

mustache = Gong Cha

salted cheese = Happy Lemon

fluffy milk tea = Little Fluffy Head

milk cap = Kung Fu Tea

creama = Teaspoon, Sharetea

sea salt creama = Plentea

HONG KONG MILK TEA

Popularly known as "silk stocking milk tea" because the sackcloth used to filter the tea resembles that of pantyhose, this is our rendition of a historic drink that can be found in every restaurant in Hong Kong. Ours is a much simpler version, but the Hong Kong original taste produces a full-bodied taste that only this authentic method of brewing can bring forth.

PREP TIME
15 minutes

Serves 1

YOU WILL NEED
Glass jar, spoon

⅛ cup (40mL) condensed milk

1 cup brewed black tea

Ice cubes

1. Put the condensed milk into a glass jar.

2. Add the brewed tea.

3. Use a spoon to mix for approximately 1 minute.

4. Add the ice cubes and enjoy.

VARIATION Experiment with evaporated milk and different black tea types for a more authentic taste.

QUICK TIP Visit Hong Kong on your next vacation to view the craftsmanship behind this notable drink and to taste the real thing!

CARAMEL MILK TEA

Taking bubble milk tea to the next sugar level, this caramel milk tea is for serious sweet-tooths only! Delicious decadence in a glass is rimmed with pure caramel drizzle topped with homemade milk foam and all the caramel you can handle! This is for you, my sugar-fiend friends!

PREP TIME
10-15 minutes

Serves 1

YOU WILL NEED
Glass jar

Caramel sauce, to taste

1 Bubble Milk Tea
  (see page 51)

½ cup (100mL) classic
  milk foam
  (see page 41)

Ice cubes

1. Drizzle caramel sauce on the rim as you rotate the glass jar.

2. Add the bubble milk tea.

3. Add the milk foam on top (or substitute whipped cream).

4. Decorate with more caramel drizzle on top of the milk foam

5. Sip and enjoy!

VARIATION Experiment with other sauces like chocolate, and so on.

DAIRY-FREE OPTION Replace the milk with an alternative milk such as oat, rice, or soy.

BEST PAIRED WITH Tapioca and mini pearls.

BROWN SUGAR MILK

The name says it all. It's a simple drink composed of brown sugar, tapioca, and milk. And to be honest with you, I wasn't always a fan. My initial reaction was "there isn't even any tea!" What I didn't know was, when made correctly and the ingredients aligned perfectly, the caramelized brown sugar intensified the milk like a syrup. Some say it tastes like cereal milk, and for me that's the best part of eating cereal!

COOK TIME
45 minutes

Serves 1

YOU WILL NEED
Glass jar, spoon,
saucepan

½ cup (80g) cooked
   brown sugar tapioca
   (see page 38)

¼ cup dark brown sugar

Ice cubes

1½ cups milk

1. Cook the tapioca with the brown sugar tapioca recipe.

2. Instead of soaking the tapioca balls in brown sugar, in a saucepan add ¼ cup of dark brown sugar and the cooked tapioca over low heat. Stir until the sugar dissolves and becomes caramelized with the tapioca (about 5 minutes).

3. Turn off the heat, add the brown sugar tapioca to a glass jar, and coat the glass jar with the molasses tapioca by turning the cup.

4. Add the ice cubes and fill the cup with milk.

5. Stir and enjoy.

Indulge
in life's
SWEETER
things.

Fruit Tea Series

Summer love is what comes to mind when I think about fruit teas. Eighty-degree weather, a walk in the park, brunch on the sidewalk—the only thing that can make this beautiful day even better is having the right refreshing drink to go along with it. Bask in the sun, rejuvenate with tea, and most of all, let love in. All of the drinks in this series are perfect for summer days.

PASSION FRUIT GREEN TEA

I can honestly say I never had a bad passion fruit green tea. It's a refreshing and tangy drink that bounces from sweet to tart and then back to sweet again. When you need a sure thing, this is your girl. Set yourself up for success. Get the passion fruit green tea.

PREP TIME
10 minutes

Serves 1

YOU WILL NEED
Glass jar,
a shaker or
mason jar

Ice cubes

¼ cup (35 mL) passion fruit syrup (such as Torani)

Simple syrup, to taste (see page 30)

1 cup brewed jasmine green tea

1. Put the ice cubes, passion fruit syrup, simple syrup, and brewed tea into a shaker or Mason jar.

2. Close the shaker or jar and shake vigorously for 30 seconds.

3. Pour the contents into a Mason jar.

BEST PAIRED WITH Jelly, aloe vera, or popping boba.

VARIATION Replace passion fruit syrup with real passion fruit pulp. The pulp from one passion fruit can make 2 drinks.

LEMON TEA

Growing up Asian, I drank my fair share of Vita® brand box drinks. My go-to would be their chrysanthemum honey tea, but all of them are tasty. And I mean all of them! This drink is inspired by their lemon tea. It's that refreshing drink on a midsummer day. As the cliche goes, when life give you lemons, crush them, and make lemon tea! Hey, you got this!

Ice cubes

½ tablespoon lemon juice

Simple syrup, to taste (see page 30)

1 cup brewed tea

1. Put the ice cubes into a glass jar.

2. Add the lemon juice.

3. Add the simple syrup.

4. Add your choice of brewed tea.

5. Stir and enjoy.

6. Add garnishes (optional, see below).

BEST PAIRED WITH Jelly or aloe vera

GARNISH Lemon slice, lime slice, mint leaves

STRAWBERRY GREEN TEA

Good in jam, better in boba—strawberries are the best. With all their health benefits, they're a super berry and the title is well deserved.

PREP TIME
10 minutes

COOK TIME
5 minutes

Serves 1

YOU WILL NEED
Blender,
glass jar

FRUIT TEA SERIES • 63

Ice cubes

¼ cup strawberry puree

Simple syrup, to taste
(see page 30)

1 cup brewed jasmine
green tea

GARNISH Diced
strawberries and a
strawberry wedge

BEST PAIRED WITH
Strawberry popping
boba

1. Put the ice cubes into a
glass jar.

2. Add the strawberry puree.

3. Add the simple syrup.

4. Add the brewed tea.

5. Stir and enjoy.

6. Add garnishes (optional,
see below).

STRAWBERRY PUREE

½ pound strawberries

⅛ cup (25g) cane sugar

⅛ cup (25g) hot water

1. Wash and hull the strawberries.

2. Put the strawberries into the blender.

3. Mix the sugar and hot water until the
sugar is dissolved.

Strawberry Pop

• Replace the tea
with sparkling water.

4. Put the mixture into the blender.

5. Start at a low speed and slowly ramp up to the desired speed for your
preferred texture.

6. Optional: Pour into an airtight container and store in the refrigerator
for up to 1 week.

LYCHEE GREEN TEA

Lychee is absolutely one of my favorite fruits. A thin outer layer of skin coats the rounded white flesh within. Just remove the skin, pit, and devour whole! Each bite bursts with natural lychee juice that keeps you wanting more. This tea combines that delicious taste with iced green tea—the perfect addition to your self-care routine.

PREP TIME
10 minutes

Serves 1

YOU WILL NEED
Blender,
glass jar

Ice cubes

Lychee puree

Simple syrup, to taste
(see page 30)

1 cup brewed jasmine
green tea

1. Put the ice cubes into a glass jar.

2. Add the lychee puree.

3. Add the simple syrup.

4. Add the brewed tea.

5. Stir and enjoy.

6. Add garnishes (optional, see below).

GARNISH 2 lychees

BEST PAIRED WITH Lychee jelly or aloe vera.

VARIATION Try with other tea options like black tea.

LYCHEE PUREE

5 lychees

1. Put the lychees into the blender.

2. Blend to the preferred texture.

PEACH LIME GREEN TEA

Fuzzy on the outside and lush within, peaches are fun to touch and heavenly to taste. The spritz of lime juice in this drink intensifies the peach flavor for a Caribbean charm. It's your stay-cation to a vacation. Life's a peach!

Ice cubes

Peach lime puree

Simple syrup, to taste
  (see page 30)

1 cup brewed jasmine
  green tea

1. Put the ice cubes into a glass jar.

2. Add the peach lime puree.

3. Add the simple syrup.

4. Add the brewed tea.

5. Stir and enjoy.

6. Add garnishes (optional, see below).

PREP TIME

10 minutes

Serves 1

YOU WILL NEED

Blender,
glass jar

FRUIT TEA SERIES • 67

 GARNISH Peach slices and a lime wedge

PEACH LIME PUREE

Half a peach

½ teaspoon lime
  juice

1. Put the peach and lime juice into the blender.

2. Blend to your preferred texture.

GRAPEFRUIT GREEN TEA

The fruit of pain and pleasure—grapefruit hits the spot with its bittersweet zing. At first bite, the sourness will tickle your tongue and then reward you with its sweet aftertaste. When combined with jasmine green tea, the floral smooths out the tartness of the fruit for a delightful balance between sour and sweet.

PREP TIME
10 minutes

Serves 1

YOU WILL NEED
Glass jar,
citrus juicer

½ grapefruit

Ice cubes

Simple syrup, to taste (see page 30)

1 cup brewed jasmine green tea

1. Use a citrus juicer to juice the grapefruit (if you don't have a juicer, you can also manually juice it).

2. Put the grapefruit juice into a glass jar.

3. Add the ice cubes.

4. Add the simple syrup.

5. Add the brewed tea.

6. Stir and enjoy.

7. Add garnishes (optional, see below).

GARNISH Grapefruit slices and a lemon slice

BEST PAIRED WITH Jelly or popping boba

Grapefruit Pop

- Replace the jasmine green tea with sparkling water.

I LOVE

you so

MATCHA.

Matcha Series

Stemming from green tea leaves, matcha is a super boost of green tea in powder form. Matcha leaves are treated more delicately than their other green tea counterparts. To acquire that radiant bright green hue, matcha leaves are specially grown and processed. Just like coffee afficionados, serious matcha enthusiasts drink it straight, reveling in its full, luscious flavor.

Don't worry though, you don't have to be a matcha enthusiast to enjoy this alluring drink. These matcha recipes are created through the lens of our beloved bubble tea, swapping the bitterness for a gentler taste. Forgive us matcha, for we crave sweets.

MATCHA LATTE

Matcha lattes are by far the most popular matcha drinks. They can be found anywhere from specialty matcha cafes to fast food chains, but not all are created equal. The quality of the matcha varies tremendously, and so will yours, depending on the matcha powder you use. The easiest way to test matcha powder is by its color—look for the bright green hue; the greener, the better.

PREP TIME
5 minutes

Serves 1

YOU WILL NEED
Glass jar

Ice cubes

¾ cup milk

Simple syrup, to taste
  (see page 30)

Matcha tea
  (see page 74)

1. Put the ice cubes into a glass jar.

2. Add the milk.

3. Add the simple syrup.

4. Slowly pour the matcha tea over an ice cube for a layered effect.

5. Stir and enjoy.

BEST PAIRED WITH Matcha tapioca

DAIRY-FREE OPTION Replace milk with alternative milk

MATCHA TEA RECIPE

This recipe is the foundation of all of our matcha drinks. Matcha tea is the bona fide way of drinking matcha, and it is traditionally consumed as part of a Japanese tea ceremony. The following recipes are more of a modern take, but we encourage you to try this time-honored method of preparation, which doesn't include milk or sugar, at least once to experience matcha in its fullest form.

PREP TIME
3 minutes

Serves 1

YOU WILL NEED
Matcha bowl,
whisk

1 teaspoon matcha
  powder

⅛ cup hot water
  (176°F/80°C)

1. Put the matcha powder in the matcha bowl.

2. Slowly pour in the hot water.

3. Whisk until the powder is dissolved (approximately 1 minute).

CHARCOAL MATCHA LATTE

Activated charcoal in the food and beverage industry is a fad that has experienced some staying power in the coffee and tea market. Charcoal is the new black—it's as simple as mixing milk and charcoal powder together! Paired with our matcha latte, it's delicious and highly Instagrammable!

PREP TIME
8 minutes

Serves 1

YOU WILL NEED
Glass jar

¼ teaspoon charcoal powder

1 teaspoon hot water

¾ cup milk

Simple syrup, to taste (see page 30)

Ice cubes

Matcha tea (see facing page)

1. Put the charcoal powder and hot water into a glass jar.

2. Stir until the charcoal powder is dissolved.

3. Keep stirring while adding the milk and simple syrup.

4. Add the ice cubes.

5. Slowly pour the matcha tea over an ice cube for a layered effect.

6. Stir and enjoy.

DAIRY-FREE OPTION Replace milk with alternative milk

MATCHA MOJITO

Mojitos are not only tasty but also entertaining to make. Activate your nose, mash the mint leaves with intention, and take in a whiff of fresh mint. This cooling sensation is therapeutic for both your mind and body.

PREP TIME
8 minutes

Serves 1

YOU WILL NEED
Glass jar,
muddler or
spoon

10 mint leaves

1 lime (cut into 4 lime wedges)

Simple syrup, to taste (see page 30)

Ice cubes

½ cup water

Matcha tea (see page 74)

1. Put the mint leaves, lime wedges, and simple syrup into a glass jar.

2. Use the muddler or back of the spoon to gently mash the mint and limes.

3. Add the ice cubes.

4. Add the water.

5. Top it off with the matcha tea.

6. Stir and enjoy.

7. Add garnishes (optional, see below).

GARNISH Elevate each sip with a whiff of mint leaves by adding more mint leaves on top of the cup.

BOBA is the answer . . . Who cares what the question is?

Special Series

In principle, any drink can be made into bubble tea. Insert any bubble tea topping into any of these recipes and they easily become bubble tea. Of course there could also be more elaborate iterations of each recipe with other toppings, but these drinks don't have to be complicated to be delicious. That's the beauty of boba! Still, sometimes it's fun to mix things up, so here are a few more novel drinks that my shop and others I've enjoyed have developed. Try them out when you feel like you want a very special boba moment to add to your day!

BOBA MOMENT

Try making your favorite non-boba drink into a bubble tea. Experiment with adding tea, milk foam, and toppings to come up with your own original recipe! What's your signature drink and topping combination?

YAKULT GREEN TEA

When I was a kid, if I had the choice between Yakult or soda, I would always choose Yakult. It's a great-tasting probiotic fermented milk drink that helps improve digestion and build immunity—but to be honest, I didn't know about the health benefits then. To the ten-year-old me, it was just a delicious treat that I devoured one after another in its 5-pack of tiny bottles. Even as a grown up, one is still not enough.

PREP TIME
8 minutes

Serves 1

YOU WILL NEED
Glass jar

Ice cubes

1–2 bottles of Yakult, to taste

Simple syrup, to taste (see page 30)

1 cup brewed jasmine green tea

1. Put the ice cubes in a glass jar.

2. Add the Yakult.

3. Add the simple syrup (I recommend adding less than you would in a normal glass of bubble tea, as Yakult is sweet on its own).

4. Add the brewed tea.

5. Stir and enjoy.

Did you know?

Each bottle of Yakult is said to contain enough probiotics to improve a person's digestion for one day. This is why Yakults are packaged in small bottles—so that they can be consumed in one sitting.

BEST PAIRED WITH
Jelly or aloe vera

STRAWBERRY MILK

Caffeine-free and kid-approved, this one takes the cake. Using a puree made with fresh strawberries, this treat is as delicious as strawberry shortcake but without the calories. #treatyourself

½ cup strawberry puree

Ice cubes

Simple syrup, to taste
  (see page 30)

½ cup milk

1. Put the strawberry puree into a glass jar.

2. Add the ice cubes.

3. Add the simple syrup.

4. Add the milk.

5. Add the garnishes (optional, see below).

6. Stir and enjoy.

STRAWBERRY PUREE

½ pound strawberries

⅛ cup (25g) cane sugar

⅛ cup (25g) hot water

1. Wash and hull the strawberries.

2. Put the strawberries into the blender.

3. Mix the sugar and hot water until the sugar is dissolved.

4. Put the mixture into the blender.

5. Start at a low setting and slowly ramp up the speed to produce your desired texture.

6. Optional: Pour into an airtight container and store in the refrigerator for up to 1 week.

Strawberry Matcha Latte

• Make strawberry
  milk and top it
  off with a
  matcha latte.

GARNISH
Strawberry wedge or
sliced strawberries

DAIRY-FREE OPTION
Replace milk with
alternative milk

STRAWBERRY LEMONADE

When simple lemonade is a little too plain, kick it up a notch with fruit purees. Strawberry is one of my favorite fruits, and it makes a great complement to this tart lemonade. The nectar of the strawberry shields us from the bitterness of the lemon juice and produces a gentler, less sour taste that keeps us craving more!

PREP TIME
10 minutes

Serves 1

YOU WILL NEED
Juicer, pitcher, glass jar

SPECIAL SERIES • 85

⅓ cup strawberry
    puree (from about
    4 strawberries)

Ice cubes

Simple syrup, to taste
    (see page 30)

¾ cup lemonade

1. Put the strawberry puree into a glass jar.

2. Add the ice cubes.

3. Add the simple syrup.

4. Add the lemonade.

5. Add garnishes (optional, see below).

6. Stir and enjoy.

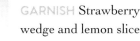

GARNISH Strawberry wedge and lemon slice

LEMONADE

¼ cup lemon juice
    (from about
    2 lemons)

½ cup simple syrup

2 cups water

1. Juice the lemons to get ¼ cup lemon juice.

2. Put the lemon juice into a pitcher.

3. Add the simple syrup and water.

4. Stir and refrigerate.

Some things
are WORTH
the weight.

Dessert Series

Although bubble tea is a treat in and of itself, let's be honest, there is no such thing as too much dessert! Pair these sweets with your bubble tea or eat them on their own to satisfy your sweet tooth. Absolutely no judgment here! This is a safe space for all your sugary compulsions.

Fun Fact

The word "desserts" is "stressed" backward! So for the sake of our mental wellness, we need to balance our lives with desserts!

PANNA COTTA

The best panna cotta I've ever had was in Taipei in the cafeteria of Google's Taiwan office. This is one of the perks of having a husband who works for Google—free lunch! Prior to that day, I had never had a good panna cotta. My husband, Ray, tried one first to make sure it was good. He was right: I loved it so much that I ended up eating three of them (and he did too!). Needless to say, I am now all about this creamy, cold treat.

In my recipe, I pair brown sugar tapioca with panna cotta for an edible version of our brown sugar milk. The original panna cotta I fell in love with had passion fruit syrup, so that's a great option too! The key is to pair your panna cotta with something sweet—and then indulge away!

PREP TIME
15 mins
CHILL TIME
4 hours

Serves 6

YOU WILL NEED
2 saucepans,
six 8-ounce cups
or any molds
of your
choice

2 tablespoons cold water

1 pack (¼ ounce) unflavored gelatin

1 ½ cups heavy cream

1 cup half-and-half

¼ cup sugar

1 teaspoon vanilla extract

1 teaspoon almond extract

2 cups (400g) cooked tapioca soaked in brown sugar syrup (see page 34)

1. Pour the cold water into a small container and slowly sprinkle in the gelatin. Let it stand for 1 minute.

2. Put the heavy cream, half-and-half, and sugar into a saucepan over medium-low heat.

3. Stir until all the sugar is dissolved and then take the pan off the heat.

4. Add the gelatin, vanilla extract, and almond extract to the saucepan with the heavy cream, half-and-half, and sugar.

5. Stir for a few minutes and let it cool.

6. Pour equal amounts into six 8-ounce cups (or the molds of your choice), shrinkwrap the top, and refrigerate for 3–4 hours or until completely set.

7. Add the cooked tapioca to each cup and enjoy.

VARIATION Replace cooked tapioca with fruit for a lighter dessert.

MAKE AHEAD Panna cotta will keep up to 3 days in the refrigerator. Add the tapioca right before serving.

MATCHA AFFOGATO

Matcha pairs well with just about everything, and ice cream is no exception. Stick with the standard vanilla ice cream to bring out the intensity of the matcha flavor, or switch it out with your favorite flavor. You can't go wrong either way!

PREP TIME
5 minutes

Serves 1

1 teaspoon matcha

2 tablespoons water (80°C)

½ teaspoon sugar

2 scoops vanilla ice cream

Sliced fruit as garnish (optional)

1. Whisk the matcha and water together in a matcha bowl.

2. Add the sugar to the matcha and whisk until it dissolves.

3. Put 2 scoops of vanilla ice cream into a bowl.

4. Pour the matcha over the ice cream.

5. Garnish with sliced fruit (optional).

YOU WILL NEED
matcha whisk,
matcha bowl,
bowl

FRUITY POPS

These popsicles bring out the fun in fruit! They're the perfect sidekick to a fruity bubble tea and a refreshing dessert for the summer. Pop them into your drinks for a chromatic effect that tastes as good as it looks.

2 mangos, peeled and sliced

2 kiwis, peeled and sliced

8 strawberries, hulled and sliced

1. Puree each type of fruit separately in the blender until smooth.

2. Fill 6 popsicle molds with equal amounts of the mango puree, followed by the kiwi puree, and then top it off with the strawberry puree.

3. Cover the mold, add the popsicle sticks, and freeze for at least 6 hours.

PREP TIME
10 minutes
COOK TIME
6 hours

Serves 6

YOU WILL NEED
blender,
six 3-ounce
popsicle molds,
6 popsicle
sticks

VARIATION Experiment with other types of fruit and add more layers for a more colorful pop!

SOUFFLÉ PANCAKE

Not your average pancake! These Japanese soufflé pancakes are so fluffy, no wonder everyone is going crazy over them. Eat them with just a pat of butter or doll them up with your favorite fruit. Savor every bite of this delicious soft sponge cake as it crumbles in your mouth because it's just that fluffy! You can get creative with your garnishes—I like them with fruit, but they're also good served under half cups of tapioca.

PREP TIME
10 minutes
COOK TIME
8 minutes

Serves 2

YOU WILL NEED
hand mixer, whisk, 2 mixing bowls, saucepan with a lid, 2 plates

2 eggs, divided

1 tablespoon milk

½ teaspoon vanilla extract

2 tablespoons all-purpose flour

½ teaspoon baking powder

2 tablespoons cane sugar

1 teaspoon cooking oil

2 teaspoons water

Butter

1. Mix 2 egg yolks, the milk, vanilla extract, flour, and baking powder in a mixing bowl. Set aside.

2. Mix 2 egg whites in another mixing bowl and use a hand mixer to whip until frothy.

3. Continue to whip while gradually adding the cane sugar. Whip until stiff peaks form.

4. Gently fold the whipped egg whites into the first mixing bowl. Don't add them all at once. Start with one third of the bowl and gradually add in the rest.

5. Place the saucepan on low heat and add the oil.

6. Scoop the batter into the saucepan so it forms 4 individual pancakes.

7. Scoop again, topping each individual pancake with a second layer. Set aside one-third of the batter for later.

8. Add 1 teaspoon of water to the empty spaces in the saucepan.

9. Cover the saucepan with a lid and set a timer for 4 minutes.

10. Uncover the lid, and using the remaining batter, add another scoop on top of each pancake.

11. Gently flip each pancake.

12. Add 1 teaspoon of water to the empty spaces in the saucepan.

13. Cover the saucepan again and set a timer for 3 minutes.

14. Place 2 pancakes on each plate with a pat of butter on top of each pancake.

15. Garnish with fruit or any other preferred topping (optional).

Friends who drink B●BA together, stay together.

Boba Party Series

Now that you have become a boba connoisseur, what better way to share your love for bubble tea than by throwing a boba party? Use the recipes in this section to make drinks for larger groups, and use your imagination to modify them. Celebrate the good times with your boba squad—cheers to finding your own imperfectly perfect version of bubble tea!

BOBA MOMENT

Share your creations with your friends and the world, because there is someone out there who will appreciate your bubble tea as much as you do! #bobagoals

"When I Grow Up"
OREO POTTED PLANT
MILK TEA

PREP TIME
25 minutes

Serves 4

YOU WILL NEED
Resealable
plastic bag

I hate to say this, but I'm a plant murderer. You know the drill—you're innocently walking in a grocery store and out of the corner of your eye you catch this beautiful majestic plant. You fall in love, so you take it home with you, with the best intentions of nurturing its beauty. But what lies ahead is a broken heart and a mistake you made one too many times. Well, not again! This plant will live forever in your heart and in your stomach! Cheers to growing up!

4 Milk Foam Drinks
(use any on pages
41–42)

8 OREO® or other
chocolate sandwich
cookies

4 mint leaves
(or any green leaves)

1. Make 4 Milk Foam Drinks.

2. Remove the cream from the cookies and put the cookies in the resealable plastic bag.

3. Crush the cookies into tiny pieces.

4. Sprinkle the crushed cookies into a layer on top of each drink.

5. Add a mint leaf to each as garnish.

BEST PAIRED WITH Tapioca or mini pearls

"Secret Garden"
FRUIT TEA WITH FRUITS

Before I went to boba school, I tried making bubble tea at home. Every time, I failed miserably. On the outside looking in as I watched my bobarista make my drink, I always thought, "Why does it look so easy for them, and why am I not able to make it taste the same? What is their secret?" Now that I'm on the other side of that question, I know the "secret" is hard work and dedication. Behind the scenes, there are people who love bubble tea so much that they have spent all their time and energy creating these drinks. I myself have spent countless months figuring out the delicate balance between tea, milk, and sugar. I put in the work so that you don't have to! So, welcome to my boba garden, and enjoy this creation!

PREP TIME

15 minutes

Serves 4

1 grapefruit

1 orange

1 lemon

1 lime

4 strawberries

4 Passion Fruit
  Green Tea drinks
  (see page 61)

1. Cut the grapefruit and orange into slices.

2. Cut the lemon and lime into wedges.

3. Cut the strawberries in half.

4. Add a slice of grapefruit, a slice of orange, 1–2 lemon wedges, 1 lime wedge, and 2 half strawberries into each Passion Fruit Green Tea drink.

VARIATION Have fun and experiment with using a different fruit tea and different fruits like pineapple, blueberries, and raspberries, and so on.

QUICK TIP Combine the fruits and fruit tea in a pitcher for easy pouring.

"We Oolong Together"
LEMON HONEY OOLONG TEA

Pun intended! Bubble tea is my bae, and even my husband, Ray, acknowledges that. My priorities are as follows: bubble tea, our dog Boba, and my husband (our dog being a close second behind the bubble tea he's named for). My perfect day is a boba run with our dog to one of my favorite shops. Because, the truth is, bubble tea represents my longest relationship—anyone else with me?

3 lemons

½ cup honey

¼ cup sugar

½ cup hot water

Ice cubes

4 cups brewed oolong tea

4 sprigs of rosemary

Gummy bears

1. Cut 1 of the lemons into 8 slices.

2. Squeeze the other 2 lemons to make lemon juice.

3. Mix together the honey, sugar, lemon juice, and hot water.

4. Divide the mixture equally into the 4 glass jars.

5. Add the ice cubes.

6. Add 1 cup brewed oolong tea to each glass jar.

7. Garnish each with 2 lemon slices, 1 sprig of rosemary, and don't hold back on the gummy bears!

VARIATION Experiment with the honey and sugar measurements. This recipe is about 75 percent sweet.

"Legend of the Blue Sea"
BUTTERFLY PEA FLOWER LEMONADE

PREP TIME
15 minutes

Serves 6

YOU WILL NEED
6 glass jars,
6 stirring
spoons

It's a pretty well-known fact that when you lose something at the beach, it's gone forever. Flashback to three years ago on the third stop of our cross-country trip, when Ray lost our car key on a beach in San Diego. He didn't realize it fell out of his pockets until after we left and went roller-skating for three hours. We backtracked and found ourselves back at the beach, which was practically deserted at high tide. The change in the waterline and the lack of familiar beachgoers made it extremely difficult to figure out where we had been sitting. Through luck and a lot of help from Ray, I was somehow able to locate the place where I'd drawn a heart in the sand for him. There it was: a key half-buried by the tide, but still there! I picked it up before it was lost forever. The moral of this story is that good things come from playing in the sand—capture that feeling with this delicious drink!

½ cup lemon juice

1 cup simple syrup
(see page 30)

4 cups water

Ice cubes

Butterfly Pea Flower Tea
(see recipe below)

1. Brew the butterfly tea. Let it steep for 6 minutes.

2. Strain the tea leaves and let the tea cool.

3. Combine the lemon juice, simple syrup, and 4 cups water to make lemonade.

4. Put the ice cubes and a stirring spoon into each of the 6 glass jars.

BUTTERFLY PEA FLOWER TEA

4 cups/1 liter hot water

1 cup butterfly pea flower tea

5. Add the butterfly pea flower tea to each jar.

6. Slowly pour the lemonade over an ice cube into each glass jar.

7. Stir with the spoon to see it change color and enjoy.

VARIATION Use a blender to break the ice cubes into tiny pieces and make slushies instead.

GARNISH Add some blue gummy whales.

Melting Ice Cube Variation
Prep time 4 hours

1. Brew the butterfly tea, following the instructions above.

2. Strain the tea leaves and let the tea cool.

3. Pour the butterfly tea into 2 ice cube trays and freeze.

4. Combine the lemon juice, simple syrup, and 4 cups water to make lemonade.

5. Put the butterfly tea ice cubes into the 6 glass jars.

6. Pour lemonade into each jar.

7. Watch the colors change as the ice cubes melt.

GOODBYE, BOBA FRIENDS

Woohoo. You did it! You are now bobarista certified. Thank you so much for joining us in our boba exploration, and I hope you had as much fun preparing these drinks as I did writing this book. This only covers a small portion of the wide scope of bubble tea, and there is so much more for you to discover. The journey starts with you!

As this book comes to an end, I challenge you to continue your boba expedition and explore to your heart's content. Your imagination is the pillar of fresh ideas and new, unconventional drinks that our community thrives on to satisfy our boba hunger. You and I know only too well that there is nothing more frustrating than being hangry over a bubble tea deficiency.

So for the love of our boba friends and ourselves, keep on experimenting! Your creation might be the next big thing needed in our bubble tea world. I look forward to seeing all your wonderful creations.

Thank you from the bottom of my heart.

Your boba friend,

Wendy

BOBARISTA CERTIFICATE

Proudly presented to

_____

It's offical! Now that you have made it through the book you can call yourself a Bobarista. Cheers to many boba beverages in your future!

_____

Date completed

Wendy Leung

Wendy Leung
Professional Bobarista

Tea Resources

Here's how I source the ingredients used in the recipes in this book. Most of your supplies can be purchased from your neighborhood grocery store. For less common ingredients, I'd recommend checking out your local Asian grocery. Chains like 99 Ranch, Hmart, and Sunrise Mart ship within the United States. Amazon is a great source for tools and dry goods if the chain option isn't available to you.

99 RANCH (Taiwanese-American supermarket chain)

For black sugar, condensed milk, exotic fruits, pre-made tapioca, tapioca powder, and tea leaves.

AMAZON

For kitchen tools, matcha tools, tapioca powder, and tea leaves.

COSTCO

For brown sugar, fruits, heavy cream, and organic cane sugar.

HMART (Korean-American supermarket chain)

For black sugar, exotic fruits, pre-made tapioca, tapioca powder, and tea leaves.

SUNRISE MART (Japanese specialty market)

For black sugar, matcha powder, matcha tools, pre-made tapioca, and tea leaves.

TRADER JOE'S

For brown sugar, cane sugar, and fruits.

WHOLE FOODS

For brown sugar, cane sugar, dairy products, alternative milk products, and fruits.

Acknowledgments

Behind every great book is a multitude of amazing people. This book is your creation as much as it is mine, so thank you so much to all the talents at Sterling Epicure: Hannah Reich, Shannon Plunkett, Jo Obarowski, Rachel Johnson, and Kevin Iwano. I want to express my gratitude especially to Kate Zimmermann who reached out to me on this project. Thank you for working so patiently with me and for the infinite guidance throughout this whole process.

Thank you to my husband, Ray, for bringing joy into my life. You make me a better person, and I am constantly in awe by your kindness and generosity. You celebrate all my wins, and you hold me up in all my falls. Without you, none of this would be possible. Thank you for always believing in me. I love you.

Thank you to my family: Christine Ma, Didi Ma, Imay Leung, Kevin Leung, Linda Chiem, Patrick Leung, Sharon Wu, Yee Leung, Yim Kwong Leung, Yuk Chun Kan, and Yuk Ling Kan. Your support means the world to me and Ray.

Thank you to my lifelong friends: Edeel Khokhar, Eileen Chen, Garrett Tam, Jenny Ko, Lisa Lam, and Rita Lau. You guys are my guinea pigs, my first customers, and at times even unpaid workers. I don't say this enough, but I am so fortunate to have all of you in my life.

Thank you to my San Francisco boba crew: Alex Mckenley Taylor, Cynthia Chu, Daniel Almaguer, Derrick Lin, Eddie Lou, Eric Joe, Khoa Nguyen, Meghan Radke, Oliver Ng, Roberto Alvarez, and Sherry Li. We shared many laughs, boba runs, and lunch breaks joking about opening a bubble tea shop. Without those conversations I might not be where I am today.

Thank you to my New York boba crew: Amanda Gaspar, Barbara Ping, Connie Tam, Eric Ho, Esther Jung, Jason Kim, Jennifer Wu, Jinhwa Seo, Josephine Zhu, Joyce Guo, Judy Nie, Karl Jude Lim, Lisa Chen, Matt Chen, Mario Beshai, Melissa Chen, Nick Wong, Nicole Gay, Olivia Szeto, Perry Boon, Priscilla Cen, Stephanie Leon (Pimentel), Suzanne Nig, Victoria Lee, and Vivian Fong. Cheers to many more boba dates!

Lastly, thank you to all the boba friends out there. One thing I've learned from opening a bubble tea shop is that boba people are the best people. I'm constantly reminded of how kind people are and how much love they can empower from sharing the same passion. Thank you for letting me share this passion with you and for letting me be a part of your boba story.

Index

A

Almond milk, about, 22
Aloe vera, as topping, 21
Amount of tea to use, 27

B

Beans, red, 21
Boba. *See* Brewing tea;
  Bubble tea
Boba party series, 95–103
    about: overview of, 95
    Legend of the Blue Sea
      (Butterfly Pea Flower
      Lemonade), 102–103
    "Secret Garden" (Fruit Tea
      with Fruits), 99
    "We Oolong Together"
      (Lemon Honey Oolong
      Tea), 101
    "When I Grow Up"
      (Oreo Potted Plant Milk
      Tea), 97
Bobarista Certificate, 106
Brewing tea
    about: by tea type, 27
    amount of tea to use, 27
    brewing process, 25–26
    steep time, 27
    sweetness text/levels,
      28–29
    temperature, 27
    using tea bags (don't
      squeeze), 27

Brown sugar milk tea, 19
Brown Sugar Syrup, 34
Brown Sugar Tapioca,
  38–39
Bubble Milk Tea, 51
Bubble tea
    anatomy of, illustrated, 18
    brewing. *See* Brewing tea
    "bubble" reference
      defined, 16
    origins and uniqueness, 17
    resources, 107
    toppings, 21
    types of, defined, 19
Butterfly pea flowers
    about: brew temperature,
      time, and amount,
      27; melting ice cube
      lemonade variation, 103
    Butterfly Pea Flower Tea,
      102
    Butterfly Pea Milk Foam,
      43
    Legend of the Blue Sea
      (Butterfly Pea Flower
      Lemonade), 102–103

C

Caramel Milk Tea, 55
Certificate, Bobarista, 106
Charcoal Matcha Latte, 75
Charcoal Milk Foam, 43
Cheese Milk Foam, 41

Cheese tea, defined, 19
Chocolate
    Cocoa Milk Foam, 42
    "When I Grow Up"
      (Oreo Potted Plant Milk
      Tea), 97
Chrysanthemum flowers,
  brewing, 27
Citrus
    Grapefruit Green Tea,
      68–69
    Grapefruit Pop, 69
    Legend of the Blue Sea
      (Butterfly Pea Flower
      Lemonade), 102–103
    Lemonade, 85
    Lemon Tea, 62
    Peach Lime Green Tea, 67
    "Secret Garden" (Fruit Tea
      with Fruits), 99
    Strawberry Lemonade, 85
    "We Oolong Together"
      (Lemon Honey Oolong
      Tea), 101
Classic Milk Foam, 41
Classic Tapioca, 32–35
Cocoa Milk Foam, 42
Creamier tea, options for, 22

D

Dessert series
    about: overview of, 87
    Fruity Pops, 91

Dessert series (*cont.*)
    Matcha Affogato, 89
    Panna Cotta, 88–89
    Soufflé Pancake, 92–93

F

Foam. *See* Milk foam
Fruit, popping boba and, 21
Fruit tea series, 59–69
    about, 19; overview of, 59
    Grapefruit Green Tea,
      68–69
    Grapefruit Pop, 69
    Lemon Tea, 62
    Lychee Green Tea, 65
    Passion Fruit Green Tea, 61
    Peach Lime Green Tea, 67
    Strawberry Green Tea, 62
    Strawberry Pop, 63
Fruit Tea with Fruits, 99
Fruity Pops, 91

G

Grapefruit. *See* Citrus
Grass jelly, about, 21
Green tea
    about: alternative milks and,
      22; brew temperature, time,
      and amount, 27; matcha
      and, 71
    Grapefruit Green Tea,
      68–69
    Lychee Green Tea, 65
    Passion Fruit Green Tea, 61
    Peach Lime Green Tea, 67
    Strawberry Green Tea, 63
    Yakult Green Tea, 81

H

Hello Always Tea
    author's story of creating,
      10–15
    creating and running, 13–15
    perspective on creation
      of, 10
    Taiwan experience, 11–12
Honey Brown Sugar Syrup, 36
Hong Kong Milk Tea, 53

I

Ice cube (tea), melting, 103

J

Jelly toppings, about, 21

K

Kiwis, in Fruity Pops, 91

L

Legend of the Blue Sea
    (Butterfly Pea Flower
    Lemonade), 102–103
Lemon. *See* Citrus
Lychee Green Tea, 65

M

Mangos, in Fruity Pops, 91
Matcha and matcha series,
    71–79
    about: matcha latte, 19;
      overview of matcha and, 71
    Charcoal Matcha Latte, 75
    Matcha Affogato, 89
    Matcha Latte, 73
    Matcha Milk Foam, 43

    Matcha Mojito, 77
    Matcha Tapioca, 36
    Matcha Tea Recipe, 74
    Strawberry Matcha Latte,
      83
Milk foam
    about: how to make, 41
    Butterfly Pea Milk Foam, 43
    Charcoal Milk Foam, 43
    Cheese Milk Foam, 41
    Classic Milk Foam, 41
    Cocoa Milk Foam, 42
    Matcha Milk Foam, 43
    Milk Foam Tea, 52
Milks, alternative options, 22
Milk tea
    about: brown sugar milk
      tea, 19; defined, 19;
      overview of milk tea
      series, 47; taro milk tea,
      19; Thai milk tea, 19
    Brown Sugar Milk, 57
    Bubble Milk Tea, 51
    Caramel Milk Tea, 55
    Charcoal Matcha Latte, 75
    Hong Kong Milk Tea, 53
    Matcha Latte, 73
    Milk Foam Tea, 52
    Milk Tea (recipe), 49
    Strawberry Matcha Latte,
      83
    Strawberry Milk, 82–83
    "When I Grow Up"
      (Oreo Potted Plant Milk
      Tea), 97
Mini pearls, 21
Mojito, matcha, 77

O

Oat milk, about, 22
Oolong tea
    about: brew temperature,
        time, and amount, 27
    "We Oolong Together"
        (Lemon Honey Oolong
        Tea), 101
Oreo Potted Plant Milk Tea, 97

P

Pancake, soufflé, 92–93
Panna Cotta, 88–89
Party series. *See* Boba party
    series
Passion Fruit Green Tea, 61
Passion fruit, in "Secret
    Garden" (Fruit Tea with
    Fruits), 99
Peach Lime Green Tea, 67
Popping boba, about, 21
Pops, fruity, 91
Pudding toppings, about, 21

R

Red beans, as topping, 21
Resources, for tea and other
    ingredients, 107
Rose Water Tapioca and
    Syrup, 37

S

"Secret Garden" (Fruit Tea
    with Fruits), 99

Simple syrup, making and
    storing, 30
Soufflé Pancake, 92–93
Soy milk, about, 22
Special series, 79–85
    about: overview of, 79
    Strawberry Lemonade, 85
    Strawberry Matcha Latte,
        83
    Strawberry Milk, 82–83
    Yakult Green Tea, 81
Steep time, 27
Steps to brewing tea, 25–26
Strawberries
    Fruity Pops, 91
    Strawberry Green Tea,
        62
    Strawberry Lemonade, 85
    Strawberry Matcha Latte,
        83
    Strawberry Pop, 63
    Strawberry Puree, 63, 82
Sweetness. *See also* Syrups
    adding sugar to tea, 30
    levels and test, 28–29
    simple syrup recipe, 30
Syrups
    about: making and storing
        simple syrup, 30
    Brown Sugar Syrup, 34
    Honey Brown Sugar
        Syrup, 36
    Rose Water Syrup, 37
    Simple Syrup, 30

T

Tapioca
    about: "bubbles" and, 16
    bubble tea definition and,
        17, 19
    mini pearls, 21
    toppings, 21
Tapioca, making
    about: overview of, 31;
        powder vs. starch, 31;
        using homemade vs.
        store-bought tapioca,
        34, 35
    Brown Sugar Tapioca,
        38–39
    Classic Tapioca, 32–35
    Matcha Tapioca, 36
    Rose Water Tapioca, 37
Taro milk tea, 19
Temperature, brewing, 27
Thai milk tea, 19
Toppings, 21–22

W

"We Oolong Together"
    (Lemon Honey Oolong
    Tea), 101
"When I Grow Up" (Oreo
    Potted Plant Milk Tea), 97

Y

Yakult, defined, 19

About the Author

WENDY LEUNG is the owner and founder of Hello Always Tea, an independent bubble tea shop in New York City. Best known for their handmade tapioca, Hello Always Tea is also distinguished by its bubble tea classes. Wendy has traveled all over Asia in search of finding her perfect cup of tea. In Taiwan, she attended boba school and learned the ins and outs of what makes a good boba. She now spends her days sharing her passion with boba friends all over the country through her online presence at hellobobafriends.com.